Selena Gomez

By Kylie Burns

Crabtree Publishing Company

www.crabtreebooks.com

Crabtree Publishing Company

www.crabtreebooks.com

Author: Kylie Burns
Publishing plan research and development:
  Sean Charlebois, Reagan Miller
  Crabtree Publishing Company
Coordinating editor: Paul Humphrey
Editors: Clare Hibbert, Kathy Middleton
Photo researcher: Clare Hibbert
Proofreader: Wendy Scavuzzo
Designer: sprout.uk.com
Series design: Ken Wright
**Production coordinator and
  prepress technician:** Michael Golka
Print coordinator: Katherine Berti

Produced for the Crabtree Publishing
Company by Discovery Books

Photographs:
Alamy: Clinton Wallace/Globe Photos/ZUMA
  Wire Service: page 5
Corbis: Splash News: pages 16, 20, 27; Brent
  Perniac/AdMedia: page 26
Everett Collection: pages 6, 10
Getty Images: Scott Pribyl/MLS: page 11;
  Christopher Polk/KCA2012: page 12; Bruce
  Glikas/FilmMagic: page 14; Lisa
  Lake/WireImage: page 23
Photoshot: Everett: page 7; Starstock: page 15;
  Alan Markfield: page 17; Face to Face: pages
  18, 25
Shutterstock: s_bukley: pages 1, 21, 22; Joe
  Seer: pages 4, 19; Helga Esteb: cover, pages
  8, 9, 13, 24; Paul Smith/Featureflash: page 28

Library and Archives Canada Cataloguing in Publication

Burns, Kylie
    Selena Gomez / Kylie Burns.

(Superstars!)
Includes index.
Issued also in electronic format.
ISBN 978-0-7787-7617-8 (bound).--ISBN 978-0-7787-7630-7 (pbk.)

    1. Gomez, Selena, 1992- --Juvenile literature. 2. Actors--United
States--Biography--Juvenile literature. 3. Singers--United States--
Biography--Juvenile literature. I. Title. II. Series: Superstars!
(St. Catharines, Ont.)

PN2287.G585B87 2012   j791.4302'8092   C2012-906834-9

Library of Congress Cataloging-in-Publication Data

CIP available at Library of Congress

Crabtree Publishing Company

www.crabtreebooks.com   1-800-387-7650

Printed in the U.S.A./112012/FA20121012

Published in Canada
Crabtree Publishing
616 Welland Ave.
St. Catharines, ON
L2M 5V6

Published in the United States
Crabtree Publishing
PMB 59051
350 Fifth Avenue, 59th Floor
New York, New York 10118

Published in the United Kingdom
Crabtree Publishing
Maritime House
Basin Road North, Hove
BN41 1WR

Published in Australia
Crabtree Publishing
386 Mt. Alexander Rd.
Ascot Vale (Melbourne)
VIC 3032

CONTENTS

Words that are defined in the glossary are in
bold type the first time they appear in the text.

Superstar

Selena Gomez is an award-winning television star, recording artist, **spokesperson**, and movie star. Today, Selena Gomez has millions of fans worldwide, and her star power shines brighter than ever.

Meet Selena

In addition to her work as a performer, Selena Gomez has devoted her time and energy to several **charitable** causes, developed a clothing line, hosted award shows, and recently launched a signature perfume. She has accomplished more in her 20 years of life than many people achieve in a lifetime!

Selena attends the Hollywood Style Awards in 2009.

LIKE MOTHER, LIKE DAUGHTER

Selena Gomez always wanted to be in show business. Her mom, Mandy, was an actor and she loved helping her rehearse her lines for the theater.

When *Wizards of Waverly Place* first **aired** on television, several media reporters called Selena "the next Miley Cyrus." At that time, Miley was the star of the popular television program *Hannah Montana*.

Selena arrives at a Miley Cyrus concert.

TV Time

Selena Gomez burst onto the scene at a young age, acting and singing in popular children's television programs. She made guest appearances on several shows, including the Disney Channel's *The Suite Life on Deck* and *Hannah Montana*. In 2007, when she was just 15 years old, the Disney Channel gave Selena a starring role in *Wizards of Waverly Place*.

She Said It

[Miley Cyrus] is obviously extremely successful, and I think she's a wonderful performer . . . So being compared to her, I was very, very flattered.
—Interview with Marc Malkin of E!Online.com, 2008

Disney Princess

Selena is most often recognized for her role on the Disney Channel's award-winning television show, *Wizards of Waverly Place*. For five years, she played the role of a young wizard named Alex Russo. She not only starred in the show, but she sang the theme song, too. Selena Gomez can do it all!

Out of This World

Wizards of Waverly Place was the Disney Channel's longest-running series. It lasted four seasons and produced 106 episodes and one TV movie. The series won an Outstanding Children's Program Emmy Award in 2009. *Wizards of Waverly Place: The Movie* also won an Emmy the following year.

The first ever *Wizards* episode, "The Crazy 10 Minute Sale," aired on October 12, 2007.

Everything Is Not What It Seems!

Selena Gomez played the middle child in a family with three wizard children on *Wizards of Waverly Place*. Selena and her character, Alex Russo, couldn't have been more different. Selena is responsible, thoughtful, and kind. Alex is outgoing, opinionated, and sometimes mean. One thing they did share, however, was a love of clothing!

Selena poses with David DeLuise, who plays Jerry Russo, her father in *Wizards of Waverly Place*.

She Said It

I don't get into as much trouble as Alex does, but I do like the Converse sneakers she always wears. Alex has kind of a funky, laid-back, individual style. I think that's something we share.

—Interview with Vickie An on timeforkids.com, 2007

Rising Talent

Selena's dress for the 2011 MTV Music Awards showed off her dark hair and eyes.

Selena Marie Gomez was born on July 22, 1992, and raised in Grand Prairie, Texas. At that time, another Texas native named Selena Quintanilla-Pérez was achieving superstar status as a singer and performer throughout the United States and Mexico. The 21-year-old was a **vibrant** brunette beauty, and an award-winning pop star. Selena Gomez's parents decided to give their newborn daughter the same name as the famous singer, Selena.

All in the Family

Selena's television family on *Wizards of Waverly Place* shares the same **heritage** as her real-life family. Selena's parents have Mexican and Italian roots, just like the Russos. Selena's father is Mexican-American, and her mother has Italian **ancestry**. The Russos are the opposite on the show. In both families, heritage plays an important role.

One and Only

Selena Gomez is an only child. Her parents were very young when she was born, and their marriage ended when Selena was five years old. Her parents are Mandy Teefey and Ricardo Gomez. Selena's mom got remarried in 2006 to Brian Teefey. They lived in Texas until Selena got her big break on *Wizards of Waverly Place*. That's when the family decided to leave Texas and move to Los Angeles, California, in 2007.

Moonlighting

Selena's mom is her manager. Mandy and Brian also run Selena's production company, July Moon Productions. Selena started the company so she could have more opportunities to choose good movie

Selena and her mom are very close.

roles. Her company is named for the month she was born and the meaning of her name. Selena comes from the Greek word for "moon."

Barney Buddies

Selena began acting at age ten when she was chosen to play the part of Gianna on *Barney and Friends*. It was during her two years on the show that Selena became best friends with another young actress, Demi Lovato.

Barney the dinosaur poses with Demi (on the blue ball wearing glasses) and Selena (on the yellow ball).

Chance Meeting

Selena and Demi auditioned along with 1,400 other young girls to win a role on *Barney and Friends*. Selena was nervous. When Demi turned around in line and asked, "Do you want to color with me?" Selena happily said "Yes." That day, the two girls became **inseparable**. Selena won the role of Gianna, and Demi won the role of Angela. They worked together again years later on the TV show *Sonny with a Chance* and in a TV movie called *Princess Protection Program*.

She Said It

[Selena and I] love watching movies [together] too, like scary movies—on Halloween we watched like so many scary movies together, it was awesome!
—Demi Lovato, in *People Magazine*, 2009

Taking It Easy

Selena Gomez may be a superstar, but she's also a regular girl with a variety of interests. She loves to spend time with her friends surfing, playing basketball, watching scary movies, and attending **NBA** games when the San Antonio Spurs are in town.

All in a Day's Work

Once, when she was asked what she did after a photoshoot for *Teen Vogue Magazine* (2012), Selena said, "We went to the house, made tacos, watched TV, and lounged." No diva behavior for this down-to-earth star!

SCHOOL ON SET

The demands of a hit show meant that Selena couldn't go to regular school. Instead, she and her co-stars on *Wizards of Waverly Place* were **tutored** on set for five hours a day.

Although she has to dress up a lot for her work, Selena says she prefers casual clothes and a ponytail.

Making a Scene

Selena Gomez loves to sing. She recorded the theme for *Wizards of Waverly Place*, did a remake of the Disney song, "Cruella de Vil," recorded songs on the *Tinkerbell* **soundtrack**, and sang on a Disney **compilation album**. Just before her 16th birthday, Hollywood Records signed Selena to a recording contract. Her band, Selena Gomez and the Scene, released their first album, *Kiss and Tell*, in 2009. *A Year Without Rain* followed in 2010, and *When the Sun Goes Down* in 2011.

It Comes Naturally

The song "Naturally" was a fan favorite. It went to Number 29 on *Billboard*'s Top 100 Songs in 2012. When it reached more than one million sales, it earned **platinum** status within the recording industry.

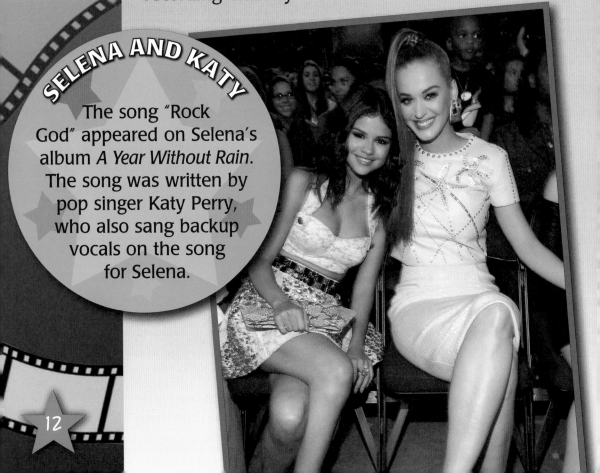

SELENA AND KATY

The song "Rock God" appeared on Selena's album *A Year Without Rain*. The song was written by pop singer Katy Perry, who also sang backup vocals on the song for Selena.

Selena and the band share a laugh at the 2011 People's Choice Awards.

Band on the Run

Not only do fans love to listen to Selena Gomez and the Scene, they love to watch them perform, too. The band have toured the world with their upbeat, techno-pop music, playing in countries such as Canada, Britain, Brazil, Mexico, and the United States. They completed three concert tours and three albums between 2009 and 2012.

ROCKIN' THE SCENE!

The Teen Choice Award for Choice Music: Group went to Selena Gomez and the Scene in 2010 and 2011. The band also won the People's Choice Award for Favorite Breakout Artist in 2011. Clearly, they have fans of all ages!

Living a Fairytale

TWINKLE TOES

Selena learned hip-hop and tango dancing for her role in *Another Cinderella Story*. She also recorded some of the songs on the movie's soundtrack.

In 2009, Selena starred in the TV movie *Another Cinderella Story* as Mary, a talented dancer who feels like an outcast. Drew Seeley played the part of Joey, her modern-day "Prince Charming." Instead of losing a glass slipper, Mary drops her MP3 player. Since Selena and Drew were pals off-screen, it was a little nerve-racking to do a kissing scene and make it look like they were in love. But that's what acting is all about!

Selena Gomez and Drew Seeley share a hug on a visit to Broadway.

14

Get with the Program

In the Disney TV movie, *Princess Protection Program*, Selena reunited with her friend, Demi Lovato. Selena plays the role of Carter, a tomboy with a secret crush and no self-confidence. Demi plays Princess Rosalinda, who is in danger because of a threat to her country. Carter's dad disguises the princess as a regular teen named Rosie and moves her in with his family to protect her. The girls don't get along at first, but eventually become close friends.

Demi and Selena

Pure Magic

On August 28, 2009, Selena appeared in a made-for-TV production called *Wizards of Waverly Place: The Movie*. More than 11 million people watched the **premiere**, making it the number-one cable television program of the year. The movie also won the 2010 Primetime Emmy Award for Best Children's Program.

A Wish Gone Wrong

In the movie, Selena's character Alex and her brother Justin must battle each other for the title of Full Wizard. The loser has to give up all wizard powers!

Selena always makes time for her adoring fans.

She Said It

The day I got my first letter from a fan, I felt like I'd been touched by an angel. I opened the note and read every single word the fan, Taylor, had to say. . . . I almost cried. I wrote her back this really long letter with an autograph to show her how sweet I thought she was.

—In *Kidz Bop: Be A Pop Star!*, 2011

Up for the Challenge

Selena loves to be challenged. After her success on television, she became interested in making the leap from TV to the big screen. Her big break came with *Ramona and Beezus*. Selena was cast in the role of Beezus, big sister to **mischievous** Ramona (played by Joey King). Selena's character is really named Beatrice, but when Ramona was little she couldn't pronounce her sister's name properly and it came out "Beezus." The movie premiered on July 20, 2010, just two days before Selena's 18th birthday.

Sisters Ramona (right) and Beezus (left) look each other in the eye.

She Said It

[Selena Gomez] works incredibly hard—she reminds me of a racehorse in that way. She knows what she wants to do, and she is happiest when she is completely immersed in her work.
—Denise Di Novi, producer of *Ramona and Beezus*, in *Cosmopolitan*, 2012

In **polo**, players hit a ball with a mallet, or club—while riding on a horse!

Grace under Pressure

Another major motion picture hit theaters in 2011 co-starring Selena Gomez. In *Monte Carlo*, Selena plays Grace Bennett, a girl from Texas who is mistaken for someone else while on a trip to Paris, France. Grace, her best friend Emma (played by Katie Cassidy), and her mean stepsister, Meg (Leighton Meester), are whisked away on a European adventure of their dreams. That is, until the truth finally comes out!

Polo Problemo!

Selena told the *New York Daily News*, "I plan to take other roles in acting that are challenging for me." In *Monte Carlo*, Selena's character, Grace, must convince everyone that she is really Cordelia, a rich British girl who plays polo. Two weeks of vocal training helped Selena nail down a British accent, but no amount of training could make her a good polo player! The script had to be re-written to accommodate her not-so-hot polo skills.

Love Songs

Being a world-famous singer and actress can have its perks. Selena has been romantically linked to cute stars including Nick Jonas, Taylor Lautner, and pop sensation Justin Bieber. But being famous can also have its drawbacks, including **paparazzi** lurking everywhere to photograph the good, the bad, and the ugly.

LUCKY IN LOVE

Selena Gomez and Justin Bieber first made their relationship public during the *Vanity Fair* Oscar Party on February 27, 2011. They were photographed arriving together arm-in-arm and all smiles.

She Said It

I'm 20. I don't take anything in my personal life too seriously. I have great friends and a solid group of people I love. I feel like everything else will come ***organically***.
—In *Teen Vogue*, 2012

Puppy Love

The media often gives star couples a nickname that blends their names together. Selena Gomez and Justin Bieber have been together long enough to earn a nickname: "Jelena." As a Hollywood power-couple, Selena and Justin have used their fame to raise awareness about some important causes affecting people, animals, and the environment. Recently, the pair adopted an adorable rescue dog named Baylor from a shelter in Justin's home country, Canada.

Justin and Selena head out to a restaurant to celebrate her 20th birthday.

Reaching Out

While filming *Princess Protection Program* in Puerto Rico, Selena was shocked to find out that there are more than 200,000 homeless cats and dogs roaming the island. She supports a charity called Island Dog, Inc., which helps to educate the public about the proper treatment of animals, and to provide food for dogs living on the beaches of Puerto Rico.

A Voice for the People

Selena Gomez uses her voice to entertain and also to inspire. When she was younger, Selena collected coins for the United Nations Children's Fund (UNICEF) each Halloween. The coins were used to help UNICEF raise money for poor and needy children around the world. In 2008, she raised more than $700,000 for UNICEF. At 17, she became the youngest UNICEF **ambassador** ever. In 2009, Selena traveled to the country of Ghana where she saw first hand the needs of many children living in extreme **poverty**.

Selena wows fans in a pink dress at the 2009 UNICEF Ball.

She Said It

I want to help encourage other kids to make a difference in the world.
—In a UNICEF press release, 2008

Destination: Safety

Selena also has been a spokesperson for several organizations that promote the importance of health, safety, and making a difference in the world. She has been involved with State Farm Auto Insurance, Borden Milk, and UR Votes Count, which encourages young people to get out and vote.

DON'T TEXT AND DRIVE

Selena takes pride in being a safe and responsible driver. She always turns her cell phone off and puts it out of sight when she gets behind the wheel.

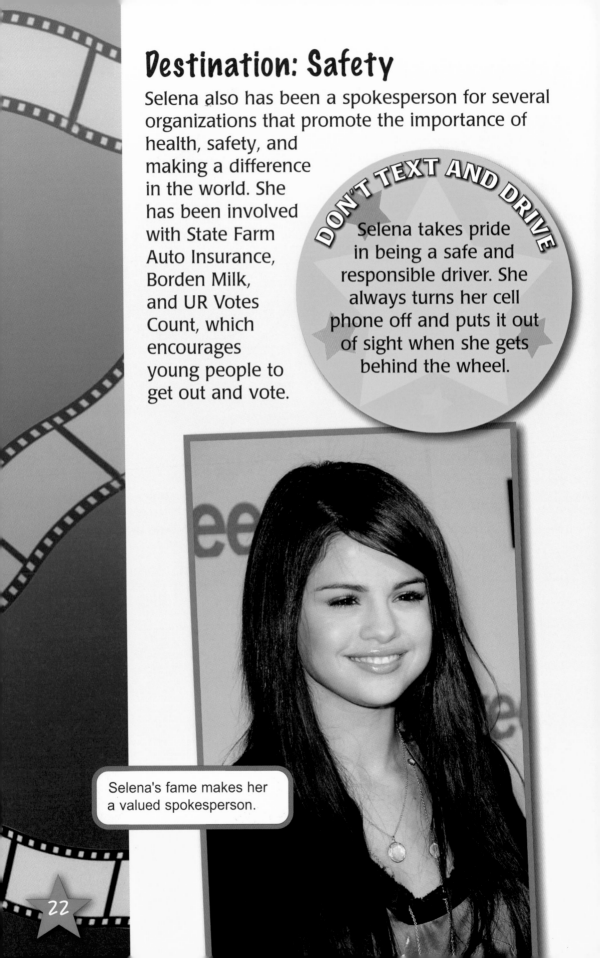

Selena's fame makes her a valued spokesperson.

Admired for her style, Selena has her own line of clothing.

Dreaming Out Loud

"Comfort," "style," and "affordability" aren't the usual words to describe Hollywood fashion, but to Selena Gomez, those words fit like a glove. She not only loves to wear comfortable clothes, she wants others to wear them, too! Her new teen clothing line, Dream Out Loud By Selena Gomez, launched in the fall of 2010. She calls her line "pretty, feminine, and **Bohemian**."

Tag—You're It!

The clothes in Selena's Dream Out Loud line are made from recycled or eco-friendly materials. The tag on each piece of clothing contains an inspirational quote, such as: "Always be yourself, there's no one better." Each tag is color-coded to indicate which pieces go well together to create a complete outfit.

Reaching for the Stars

Selena Gomez is all grown up. She is beginning to take on roles that are more **mature**. On Forbes.com she was named one of the Top 10 Breakout Stars of 2008, and she has worked hard to establish herself as a respected movie star ever since.

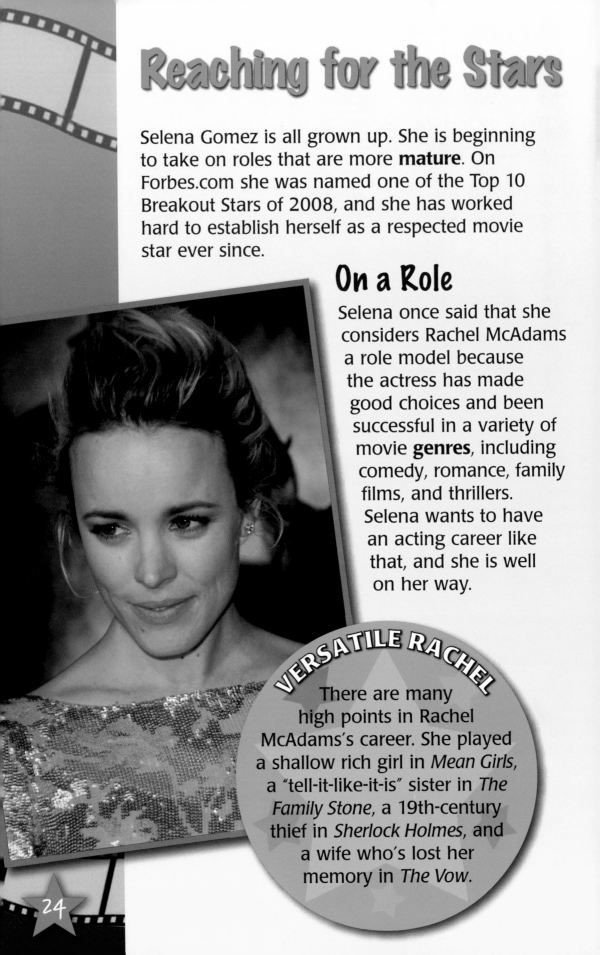

On a Role

Selena once said that she considers Rachel McAdams a role model because the actress has made good choices and been successful in a variety of movie **genres**, including comedy, romance, family films, and thrillers. Selena wants to have an acting career like that, and she is well on her way.

VERSATILE RACHEL

There are many high points in Rachel McAdams's career. She played a shallow rich girl in *Mean Girls*, a "tell-it-like-it-is" sister in *The Family Stone*, a 19th-century thief in *Sherlock Holmes*, and a wife who's lost her memory in *The Vow*.

A still from *Hotel Transylvania*, in which Selena voiced the part of Mavis (left).

Rewind!

Selena is not entirely out of the children's film industry just yet, however. In 2012, she provided the voice of one of the main characters in the 3D-animated movie *Hotel Transylvania*. She plays Mavis, the 118-year-old daughter of Dracula. She had done voice work for animation before. In 2008, she provided the voice for the mayor's daughter Helga, in *Horton Hears a Who*.

Bad Blood

Hotel Transylvania tells the story of Mavis's dad who wants to protect his daughter from falling in love with an outsider. The outsider is a boy named Jonathan. When Jonathan stumbles into Dracula's monster resort, he falls in love with Mavis, angering Dracula.

Hit the ... Pause!

In January 2012, Selena announced that her band, Selena Gomez and the Scene, were parting ways, at least for a while. Selena had a busy movie schedule ahead, and she didn't want her band members to miss out on other opportunities. After making three albums in three years, she felt it was time to put her energy into her growing film career.

The world hasn't seen (or heard) the last of Selena Gomez and the Scene.

Movie Machine

Wanting to grow beyond her image as a child actor, Selena chose three very different grown-up roles for her next film projects. In the 2012 movie *Spring Breakers*, she plays a college girl who gets into trouble when she and three friends steal some money so they can go to Florida for a vacation. Next, Selena will be seen in the black comedy *Feed the Dog* which tells the story of a crazy rock-and-roll road trip. Closing out 2013, Selena will play a woman on the run, with Ethan Hawke, in the action-thriller *Getaway*.

PARENTAL GUIDANCE

Younger fans of Selena will not be able to see some of her newer movies because they are rated for viewers 18 years or older. Selena's fans mean a lot to her, and she is careful in her social networking to give warnings if any of her projects may not be appropriate for younger fans.

Selena and co-star Ashley Benson take time out for some fun during the filming of *Spring Breakers*.

Go, Miss Gomez!

After a busy year of filmmaking, Selena is turning her interest back to music. In June 2012, she said she hoped to get back to writing songs, recording a new album, and touring soon. Her musical tastes these days include Jason Mraz and Parachute. A smart businesswoman, Selena also made time to launch a perfume in 2012 named after herself. But acting is still her passion, and this multitalented performer hopes to have a long career ahead of her.

Selena blows a kiss to her cheering fans.

She Said It

I'd like my music career to keep growing, start a prime-time weekly sitcom and make dramatic films with some first-rate directors. ...I'd love to be part of another ensemble series—something contemporary and kooky and funny and a bit romantic. Like Friends *was back when it started. ...The two [film] directors I'd really like to work with the most are David Fincher and Martin Scorsese. A little crazy? Maybe, but I can dream, can't I?*

—In an interview with Toronto.com, January 2012

Timeline

1992: Selena Marie Gomez is born on July 22 and then raised in Grand Prairie, Texas

1997: Selena's parents divorce

2001: Selena lands the role of Gianna on *Barney and Friends*

2006: Her mother Mandy remarries

2006: She guest-stars on the Disney Channel's *The Suite Life on Deck* and *Hannah Montana*

2007: Selena is cast to play Alex Russo, on Disney's *Wizards of Waverly Place*

2008: She stars in the movie *Another Cinderella Story*

2008: Selena Gomez and the Scene sign a recording contract with Hollywood Records

2009: They release their first album *Kiss and Tell*

2009: Selena films *Wizards of Waverly Place: The Movie* and *Princess Protection Program*

2009: Selena Gomez becomes the youngest ambassador for UNICEF

2010: Selena Gomez and the Scene win the Teen Choice Award for Choice Music: Group

2010: Selena co-stars in the motion picture *Ramona and Beezus*

2010: Selena launches her Dream Out Loud clothing line

2011: Selena co-stars in the motion picture *Monte Carlo*

2011: Her band wins the same Teen Choice Award for the second year in a row, as well as the People's Choice Award

2012: Selena Gomez and the Scene call it quits—for now

2012: She provides the voice of Mavis in the animated film *Hotel Transylvania*

2012: Selena takes on roles in *Spring Breakers*, *Getaway*, and *Feed the Dog*

Glossary

aired When a program is first shown on TV

ambassador The representative of an organization or country

ancestry A family's history, including where it came from

Bohemian Unconventional in style

charitable Describes something to do with charity— in other words, something to benefit others

compilation album A collection of songs by various artists

genre The particular style of a book, show, or film

heritage The beliefs and traditions passed down through the generations

inseparable Together all the time

mature Fully grown or adult

mischievous Always creating trouble

NBA The United States' National Basketball Association

organically Naturally, without any artificial interference

paparazzi Photographers who make a living by selling photographs of famous people

platinum The award given to a music group or singer when a recording reaches one million sales

polo A horseback sport, in which players use long-handled mallets to hit the ball through goalposts

poverty The state of having little or no food or money

premiere The first public performance of a movie, show, or musical performance

soundtrack An album of the music that is featured in a movie or television show

spokesperson Someone who speaks to the public about a cause they support

tutored Taught outside of a traditional classroom setting, usually one-on-one or in a small group

vibrant Lively or full of life

Find Out More

Books

Brooks, Riley. *Selena Gomez* (All Access). New York: Scholastic Inc., 2009.

Edwards, Posy. *Selena Gomez* (Me & You). London, England: Orion Publishing, 2011.

Potts, Kimberly. *Kidz Bop: Be A Pop Star!* Avon, MA: F&W Media, 2011.

Williams, Zella. *Selena Gomez: Actress and Singer.* New York: Rosen Publishing, 2011.

Websites

Selena Gomez Online
 www.selenagomez.com
Selena's official website

Selena Gomez & the Scene
 www.myspace.com/selenagomez
Selena's awesome blog spot

The Disney Channel Website
 www.disney.go.com
Hosts the *Wizards of Waverly Place* home page

UNICEF
 www.unicef.org
The organization for which Selena is
an ambassador

Index

About the Author

Kylie Burns is a part-time freelance writer and a full-time teacher. She has written children's books on a variety of cool topics, including science, sports, character education, math, and history. She feels grateful to teach children all day—then write for them at night! At home, she has three great kids, a supportive husband, and one very demanding guinea pig.